A Day
on a
Shrimp Boat

A Day
on a
Shrimp Boat

By Ching Yeung Russell

With photography by
Phillip K. Russell

Sandlapper Publishing, Inc.

*Special thanks to Captain Bob Upton
for his generous help with this project.*

FIRST EDITION 1993

Published by Sandlapper Publishing, Inc.
P.O. Box 730, Orangeburg, SC 29116-0730
MANUFACTURED IN THE UNITED STATES OF AMERICA

The typeface for *A Day on a Shrimp Boat* is Korinna.
Design by BLJ Publishing Resources, Inc.
Printed by

Library of Congress Cataloging-in-Publication Data

Russell, Ching Yeung, 1945-
A day on a shrimp boat / by Ching Yeung Russell ;
with photography by Phillip K Russell. — 1st ed.
p.   cm.
Summary: A true-to-life account of a typical day
in the life of a shrimp boat crew working off the
South Carolina coast.
ISBN 0-87844-120-4
1. Shrimp fisheries—South Carolina—Atlantic
Coast—Juvenile literature. 2. Shrimpers (Persons)—
South Carolina—Atlantic Coast—Juvenile literature.
[1. Shrimp fisheries. 2. Shrimpers (Persons)]
I. Russell, Phillip K., 1946-   ill.   II. Title.
SH380.62.U6R87 1993
639'.543'09757—dc20   93-8899
                                                     CIP
                                                     AC

A Day

My name is Jeremy. That's me (in the middle) with my father, Phillip K. Russell, who took the photographs in this book, and my brother Jonathan.

And this is my mother, Ching Yeung Russell, who wrote this book.

We wanted to see how a shrimper gets shrimp. During the Thanksgiving holiday, Dad arranged for our family to go out on Captain Bob Upton's shrimp boat, the *Abbie R.*, for a day's catch.

We had to leave our home at 3:00 a.m. to get to Frogmore, South Carolina by 5:00 in the morning. It was still dark. There were about sixteen shrimp boats at the same dock. Some of the other boats were also preparing for their day's work. The air smelled like dead fish and shrimp.

A Day

When we got on board, I asked Captain Bob why he had to go to work so early. He said that 5:00 a.m. was not that early! In the summer, he has to start at 4:00 a.m., because there is a law in South Carolina that commercial shrimpers can only shrimp from half an hour before daylight until half an hour after dark. By the time the boat travels from its dock in the tidal creek to the ocean, it is about time to lower the nets into the water. At low tide and when the tides turn are the best times for shrimping.

Captain Bob has been shrimping for thirty-two years. On his seventy-foot-long shrimp boat, he works twelve to fourteen hours a day, six days a week during the shrimping season, which in South Carolina is the months of June through December. When it is not shrimping season in South Carolina, Captain Bob sometimes takes his boat to the Gulf of Mexico or as far as Key West, Florida, to shrimp. If he doesn't go to Florida, he just stays at home and trawls for crabs and conchs in winter and spring.

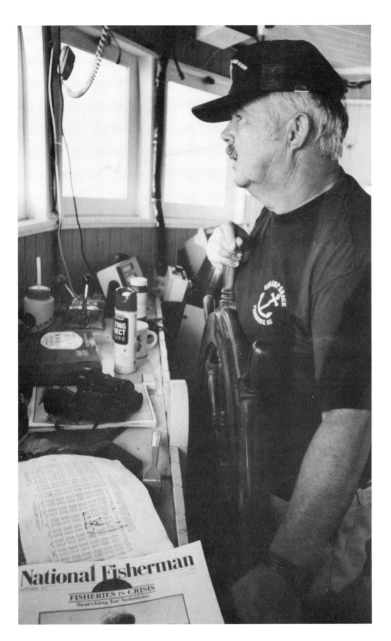

on a Shrimp Boat   5

In some ways, the shrimp boat is very much like other boats. Below the deck is the engine room. The part above deck is the cabin. It has a kitchen (called a "galley"), with a sink, stove and table. The kitchen also has a television set, for entertainment and information. The cabin has two bedrooms and a bathroom. At the front of the cabin is the wheelhouse, where Captain Bob steers the boat.

A Day

On the deck are winches, cables, chains, ropes, and nets. This equipment can be confusing to outsiders.

on a Shrimp Boat

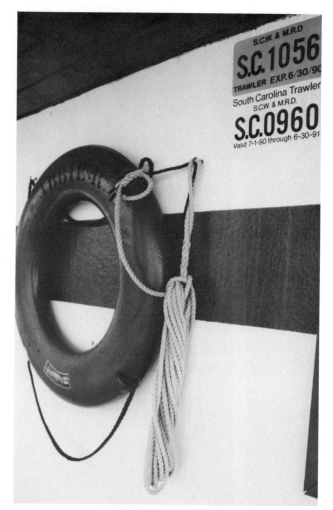

Every shrimp boat is required to have a shrimping license that must be renewed annually. When Captain Bob sails into the Gulf of Mexico or to Key West, he has to buy another license to be able to shrimp in those waters. A shrimper who gets caught shrimping with an expired license has to pay a fine and may also have his shrimping license taken away for thirty days.

A Day

The weather is very important to everyone who works on the sea. Before he starts his day's work, Captain Bob listens to the marine radio to see what the weather will be. He also has checked the forecast the night before on TV.

In recent years, shrimpers have had to add devices to their boats and nets for their own safety and to protect the endangered sea turtles. Each boat now carries a homing device, which is located on the outside of the ship's cabin. If the boat sinks at sea, the homing device will send up a signal to a satellite, giving the boat's identity and its location so that Coast Guard rescuers can find the boat and rescue its crew.

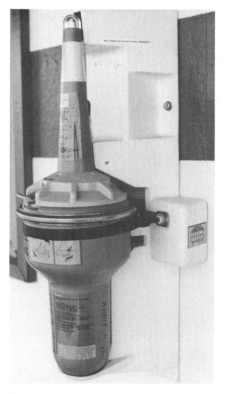

Shrimpers also have to equip their nets with turtle excluder devices (called TEDS for short) that allow sea turtles to escape from the nets. TEDS help save the sea turtles, but they also can cause the shrimpers to lose up to twenty percent of their catch. This hurts the shrimpers' profits.

Captain Bob introduced us to Bubba and Tommy, his crew. The crew members on a shrimp boat are called strikers. Bubba and Tommy work very hard because the catch is unpredictable and they get a percentage of the day's catch instead of a salary. If it is a good catch, their share is pretty good; if not, they have a bad day, too. Strikers on most of the shrimp boats in the area get a percentage of the catch instead of a salary.

on a Shrimp Boat

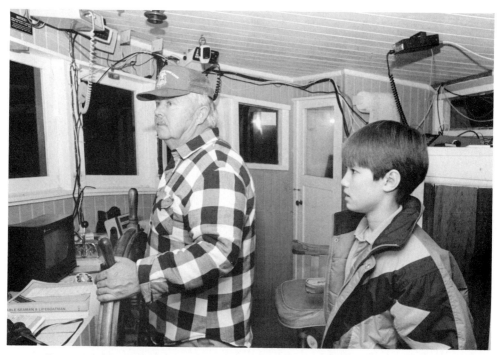

Soon after we boarded the boat, Captain Bob started the engine. Bubba and Tommy got ready to cast off. The strong smell of diesel fuel came up from the engine room below the deck.

When the *Abbie R.* started moving, I went to the wheelhouse and watched Captain Bob steer the boat. It was dark everywhere, except for the lights from other shrimp boats in the distance.

After a while I got bored. I went inside the cabin and watched TV with my brother Jonathan. After the boat started, Bubba and Tommy had nothing to do, so they rested in their bunks.

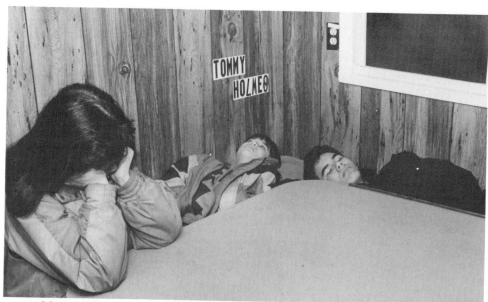

Not long afterwards, the water got choppy and the boat began to jump up and down. I felt sick to my stomach, and so did Mom. I felt so bad that I was sorry we had come on the boat, and I decided shrimping was no fun after all. There was nothing to see and nothing to do.

Dad told us to lie down. We did, and I felt better after I threw up. After a while, I fell asleep.

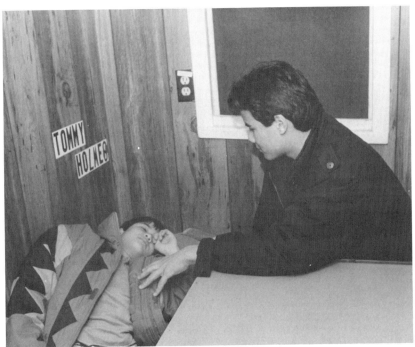

Then suddenly someone was shaking me to wake me up. It was Jonathan. He told me the boat had been moving for an hour and Tommy and Bubba were about to lower the shrimp nets. I got up and went on deck.

Bubba and Tommy lowered the outriggers, which look like wings stretched out on each side of the boat. The boat's huge shrimp nets are attached to the ends of the outriggers.

A Day

I noticed two big boards on top of the nets. I asked Captain Bob what they were for. He said they were called doors. They help to spread open the nets, which are shaped like Vs, so that the nets can cover more space.

As the *Abbie R.* traveled up and down along the coast, the shrimp nets were dragged about thirty feet behind the boat and several feet above the ocean floor. The nets catch the shrimp as the boat sails along.

I asked Bubba when they were going to raise the nets. He said it would take about an hour.

Although Bubba and Tommy could move around on the boat and even take short rests, Captain Bob stayed in the wheelhouse to steer the boat. Sometimes he talked into the marine band radio and exchanged information with the other shrimpers, or just had conversations with them.

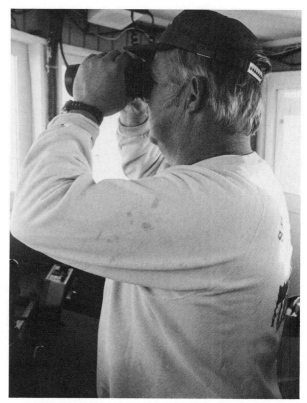

Sometimes he looked through binoculars to see the numbers on buoys.

At times he looked at the screen of the depth recorder, a machine that tells how deep the water is at the boat's location. He also checked his radar, which tells him where the coastline and shallow underwater areas are.

After the nets had been dropped for about an hour, Bubba and Tommy began to pull up a small "try net" every twenty minutes to test how many shrimp had been caught. They dropped the catch onto the deck, then picked up all the shrimp and counted them to see whether it was time to pull up the big net. If there were rocks or too many small fish in the net, Captain Bob would have to sail away from that area as quickly as possible.

The first time there were only fourteen shrimp in the try net—not nearly enough shrimp to pull up the big nets.

on a Shrimp Boat 23

After that we had to wait again, while Bubba and Tommy checked the try net every twenty minutes. Captain Bob must have noticed that I was feeling bored. He told me to come to the wheelhouse, where he taught me how to steer the boat.

About 45 minutes later, I heard a clanging sound. The engine stopped. Captain Bob told me to go back on deck and watch. Tommy and Bubba were raising the big nets!

The winch pulled up the heavy nets, which looked like four full mesh bags, and lowered them over the culling table on the deck.

Then Bubba and Tommy untied the ropes at the bottom of the nets and dropped the catch on the culling table, which was about the size of a ping pong table.

on a Shrimp Boat

Boy! I had never seen so many sea creatures before! They were blue, pink, red, grey, brown, and silver, and they dazzled my eyes. We all perked up—especially mom, who is a real seafood lover.

I thought that shrimp nets caught mostly shrimp, but in this catch there were lots of small fish, some big fish, crabs, squid, conchs, sand dollars, and horseshoe crabs. Bubba said that in warm weather they often caught baby sharks and starfish, too. The pink and grey shrimp were all mixed up with the other sea creatures.

on a Shrimp Boat

As soon as the big nets were dropped back into the water and the boat sailed on, Bubba and Tommy started to sort out the catch, using metal scrapers to pull the shrimp closer to them at the end of the culling table. They sorted the biggest shrimp into one basket and the smaller shrimp into another. Before throwing the big shrimp into the basket, they pinched the heads off.

When they had finished sorting the catch, Bubba and Tommy scraped all the shrimp heads and the other creatures—including small fish, conchs, and crabs—back into the water.

A Day

I was wondering why there was so much noise all of a sudden, when Jonathan told me to look at the water. A flock of seagulls and pelicans were following us. Some of them swooped down to peck at the surface of the water, while some skillfully caught the culls in the air. I was fascinated by those noisy, hungry, happy birds.

A Day

 Because she loves sea-food so much, Mom couldn't stand seeing all those sea creatures being thrown back into the sea. She asked Bubba if she could keep the squid and some of the crabs. Bubba said she could help herself. He even volunteered to put some of the crabs in a box for her. I hadn't seen Mom that happy since she got on the boat. By the end of the day, she had collected several pounds of squid and several dozen crabs. She said it was worth even being seasick. After all, she hadn't had any fresh squid to eat since she came to the United States!

Mom asked Bubba if we could help to sort out the shrimp. He said yes. She picked up one of the shrimp to show me. It looked weird with its head on. It had shiny little bug eyes that seemed to be staring at me. I was scared, because it was the first time in my life I had been so close to a live shrimp. All the shrimp I had seen before that day were in the grocery store, dead and headless.

Mom encouraged me to touch the shrimp.
I was afraid the "horn" on its head would
hurt me, until Jonathan assured me that it
wouldn't hurt me if I didn't touch its head.
I picked one up and asked Dad to take my
picture in a hurry, so I could show my
friends that I actually held a live shrimp.

on a Shrimp Boat

Bubba had a basket of shrimp with their heads still on. He put the handle of his scraping tool into the basket, swirled it around and came up with a large bundle of shrimp, all hanging together from their whiskers. Then he did it again and held up the two big bundles of shrimp. It was amazing!

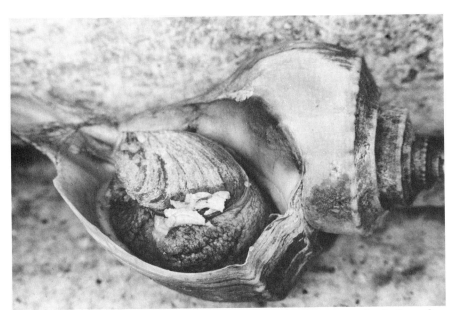

Later I found several conchs and a sand dollar for myself. I wanted to show them to my class, then put them in my collection. Mom said she would boil the conchs and eat them, but I could have the shells. I wondered why the sand dollar was green, not white like the ones I had seen in gift shops at the beach. Captain Bob told me that the sun bleaches sand dollars white when they wash up on the beach.

Jonathan found two big, funny-looking fish in the catch. Even Mom and Dad didn't know what they were. Bubba said they were sturgeons, the fish that the eggs (called roe) come from that are used to make caviar. Bubba showed us the sturgeon's funny mouth, which extends like a funnel down below its head, to suck up food from the ocean bottom.

A Day

Jonathan wanted to save one to show to his science class, but Bubba said they were a protected species. Jonathan had to let them go back to the water after Dad took his picture. I was too scared to touch them!

on a Shrimp Boat

Dad found a different kind of shrimp, called a mantis shrimp. It had a hard skeleton and little flippers all down its belly that fluttered back and forth. It looked a little scary, but Dad picked it up and it didn't hurt him.

As soon
as Bubba and
Tommy had
finished sort-
ing out the
shrimp, Tommy carried them down to the hold, the
lower part of the boat. He shoveled crushed ice on top
of the shrimp to keep them from spoiling. Meanwhile,
Bubba cleaned the deck and the culling table with a
big hose and got it ready for another load of shrimp.

Behind the boat, several pelicans still waited patiently, floating on the water and hoping we would throw out more scraps.

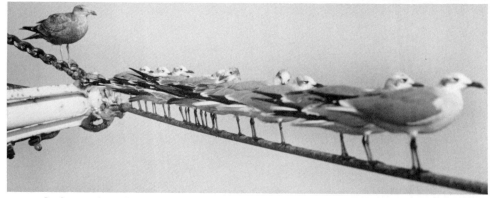

I thought the seagulls would leave us when the table was clean and we started dragging the nets again. But some of them landed on the outrigger cable and let the boat carry them. They looked very peaceful and relaxed against the blue sky. I told Dad to take their picture. He agreed, saying it would make a very artistic photo.

A Day

While we were waiting for another load of shrimp, which took about an hour, Captain Bob let me steer the boat all by myself without even watching me. I felt like a real sea captain!

Jonathan asked Captain Bob how many loads of shrimp he usually got in a day. Captain Bob said that on most days they pulled up five or six loads of shrimp and would get an average of 300 pounds in a day. On a really good day, he has caught up to 2,000 pounds—but that was about twenty years ago when the shrimp were more plentiful.

"Whaah! Are you rich, Captain Bob?" I asked, because shrimp are very expensive in the grocery store.

A Day

Captain Bob laughed. "Well, you may think that I should be rich," he said. "I have raised and supported my family by shrimping. But I have a lot of expenses. I have to make the boat payments and keep the boat up. I have to pay for insurance. I have to pay for the fuel we burn, about ten gallons an hour, and I have to pay my strikers. I have to watch the weather to see if I can go out to work. We can't catch as many shrimp as we did years ago, because there are more restrictions on shrimping. And shrimp prices have fallen, because we have to compete with imported shrimp, but insurance and fuel prices have gone up. Even though shrimping is getting harder, I still consider myself rich, because I like what I'm doing, I like being my own boss, and I like working on the water. So I think I'm rich in some ways."

A Day

When the second load was being pulled up, Captain Bob noticed something wrong with one of the doors. It had flipped upside down. I asked Captain Bob why it did that. He said sometimes the boards got stuck in the mud and flipped when they pulled loose, or sometimes the tide could flip them, but it didn't happen very often.

The board had to be returned to its proper position, otherwise the net would not stay spread. Bubba climbed out to the end of the outrigger to fix it.

It took quite a while to fix the door. Captain Bob decided to call it a day, since the day's catch was not as big as in the summer. It would cost more for fuel to continue dragging than the shrimp would be worth.

On the way back to the dock, we had to go through a bridge that swung open so we could go through. It was awesome! I had never been on a boat when it went through an open bridge.

After the boat docked, Bubba and Tommy cleaned out all the small fish and crabs from the shrimp nets and washed them with a hose. They also cleaned the deck and table. Then Bubba took the shrimp out of the hold and washed the ice away so the shrimp could be weighed.

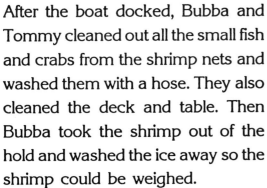

on a Shrimp Boat

Like the rest of the shrimpers around that area, Captain Bob sells his shrimp to a seafood wholesaler located right on the dock. The price Captain Bob gets from the wholesaler is much less than what we buy shrimp for at the grocery store, because the wholesaler and the grocery store have to make a profit, too. That's why Captain Bob does not make as much as I thought.

Wholesalers pack their seafood and ship it to grocery stores and to breaders and packers all over the United States. This wholesaler has a retail seafood market right at the dock. Local people who know when the trawlers return come here to buy the freshest seafood.

Captain Bob also owns a seafood restaurant, called the Shrimp Shack, just a few hundred yards from the dock. He uses some of the shrimp he catches for the restaurant, so they are really fresh there!

When we said goodbye to Captain Bob, Dad told us to stand next to the name of the boat and he took our picture. Captain Bob asked me if I would like to come back again. I hesitated for a second. I thought about how boring the day had been in the beginning and how miserable I had been when I was seasick.

I thought about how peaceful and quiet the seagulls looked on the cable, against the blue sky.

A Day

But I also thought about how amazing the catch was when it was dumped from the nets onto the table, how fascinating it was to watch the seagulls and pelicans trying to get their food. I couldn't experience those things from a textbook at school. So I said, "Yes, I'll be back!"

Ching Yeung Russell was born and raised in China and later moved to Hong Kong. She has a B.A. degree in Chinese literature and was a freelance writer while she was a student. After teaching one year at a junior high school, she married and immigrated to the United States. Her curiosity inspired her to write this book, for which her husband, Phillip Russell, took the photographs. Ching Russell's second book, *First Apple*, will be published in 1994 by Boyd's Mill Press. She and her family live in South Carolina, where she devotes her time to her family and to writing, both in English and in Chinese.

Phillip K. Russell worked as a photographer for his graduate school alumni publication and has had photographs published in two national magazines. He has traveled widely for business and pleasure, and he especially enjoys travel photography. He has collaborated with his wife on several children's picture books.